WISE
CHOICES

C000130255

A cup of
cold water

JULIA JONES

*'Get wisdom, get understanding; do not forget my words
or swerve from them.
Do not forsake wisdom, and she will protect you; love her,
and she will watch over you.
Wisdom is supreme; therefore get wisdom.
Though it cost you all you have, get understanding.'*

Proverbs 4:5-7

DayOne

© Day One Publications 2006   First printed 2006

All Scripture quotations are taken from the New International Version

A CIP record is held at The British Library   ISBN 1 84625 020 X

Published by Day One Publications Ryelands Road, Leominster, HR6 8NZ

☎ 01568 613 740 FAX 01568 611 473 email—sales@dayone.co.uk www.dayone.co.uk

Editor: Suzanne Mitchell

Design and Art Direction: Steve Devane Illustrations: Susan LeVan and Steve Devane   Printed by Gutenberg Press, Malta

A word from the publishers

Life is full of choices—and, at times, it can be easy to make the wrong ones. What a person believes influences his or her behaviour.

The Bible provides many examples of people who believed right, and whose lives, as a result, were useful.

Exercising hospitality is—in many respects—a choice to be made. It takes us out of our comfort zones; it puts pressure on times that might otherwise be spent on doing things that seem to us to be more 'important'; it may have a financial implication. Yet it is a wonderful way of putting into practice the words of the Apostle Paul: 'Be joyful in hope, patient in affliction, faithful in prayer. Share with God's people who are in need. Practise hospitality.' (Romans 12:12, 13)

For readers who do not live in the United Kingdom…

The following list should help to explain some words which I have used in this book and which might otherwise cause confusion:

Biscuit cookie

Crumble a pudding consisting of fruit covered with a topping made of a crumbly flour and fat mixture

Takeaway a hot meal bought from a shop or restaurant that is ready to be taken away and eaten elsewhere

Tea (to refer to a meal, not a drink) a light afternoon/early evening meal consisting of tea to drink, sandwiches and cakes

Teacake a light yeast-based sweet bun with dried fruit, typically served toasted and buttered

Trifle a cold dessert of sponge cake and fruit covered with layers of jelly, custard and cream

Introduction

Even if you'd make the perfect contestant for the British TV show 'Can't cook, won't cook', this book is still for you. Lack of culinary ability is probably one of the commonest objections to getting involved in giving hospitality. My hope is that as we look at this subject you will see that food plays only a small part. Rather, as the title indicates, hospitality can be as simple as tea and biscuits, or a cold drink on a hot day. Hospitality is about a willingness to share our homes and our lives with one another, rather than the ability to cook a gourmet dinner or even cope with the challenge of coordinating hot beans with toast!

Hospitality tends to be given a low priority as it's not seen as being of any great importance or effectiveness in the kingdom of God. But I believe it is vital for the healthy life of a local fellowship. We live in a society that increasingly tends towards being individualistic and fragmented. Any real sense of community, belonging or acceptance is alien to many. Think about individuals, perhaps those who live alone, or who are on the fringe of church life. Many of these will have no meaningful contact with other Christians apart from church services or meetings. So what do we do? Perhaps we try to include some 'fellowship events' in the church timetable. We may term these 'fellowship' meetings or events but often they're little more than polite and pleasant chit-chat. Often they don't achieve the aim of really getting to know one another and engaging at a deeper level. The early Christians met together daily and so could share as each had need. Often we don't really know one another well enough even to be aware when there *is* a need, be it practical, emotional or spiritual. Lovely as it might be to meet with one another daily, in most cases it's probably not feasible in twenty-first century life. So, even if we can't have the regularity of daily times together, we need to take and make other opportunities to engage with one another. We need to work on ways that will help us to get to know one another better so that we can both encourage one another and bear one another's burdens. Hospitality is a significant way of developing real fellowship. Through hospitality, relationships between Christians can be deepened. Conversely, if hospitality is not happening, these relationships may become considerably weaker.

Look at how Paul describes the church as a body in 1 Corinthians 12:24-25:

'God has combined the members of the body ... so that there should be no division in the body, but that its parts should have equal concern for each other.' It is unthinkable that a body would function effectively if the body-parts weren't aware of one another, didn't feel one another's pain, or appreciate one another's comfort. As church fellowships, we may be trying to work together on ambitious projects, long-term commitments, or running groups in the church, yet we hardly know each other. When we are involved in hospitality, we are developing relationships with those of whom God has called us to be a part.

Hospitality can also have a great impact on non-Christians, whether they are family members, friends, work colleagues or neighbours. These people can experience an acceptance in the Christian home that they wouldn't experience in any other area of life. They can discover that they are valued just because of who they are. Society offers acceptance that is conditional on such things as looks, status or achievement. The Christian values each individual as a part of God's creation, made in his image. This servant ministry of hospitality can be a powerful picture of the acceptance of a loving God. I think back to a teenage girl we knew. Her background was one without much love, in which she had only been valued if she seemed useful and she had faced much hurt and rejection. We could have spent hours talking through her problems, encouraging her to see that God loved her. Inviting her into our home frequently and regularly spoke more than words. It made real the message she heard in church, a message of love, forgiveness and acceptance. This mundane, practical service became the vehicle for God's love to impact her life.

So we see that hospitality isn't about cooking, but about communication and community. It's about opening up our homes to one another and sharing what we have and who we are.

Hospitality, as a ministry in the life of the church, can have a great effect on many lives, yet it's something we don't hear much about. It seems little has been written on the subject. It's often viewed as 'just hospitality' and, as such, is a subject that has a very low profile. Yet, as we will see, the Bible teaches that to practise hospitality should be a part of our Christian lives and an out-working of our faith. Also, it is one of the qualifications for anyone who is to serve in a leadership role in the church.

Perhaps it's sidelined because we don't recognize the position hospitality has in Scripture, or because we haven't really experienced it enough personally. Or it could be that we just take it for granted that some people are good at hospitality, so they should carry on with that task while others do what they're good at. We know who'll be asked if the visiting speaker needs feeding, or somewhere to stay overnight, so we can relax on that count as others exercise their gift. I believe that there are indeed those who do have the particular gift of hospitality, but I also believe all of us should be getting on with the practice of it. Who knows, as we practise, we may even find we get better!
We will be exploring these issues more fully in the following chapters.

Hurdles to hospitality
—why is hospitality hard?

THE DRAWBRIDGE MENTALITY—WE LIVE IN AN ISOLATED AND ISOLATING SOCIETY

Many of us are used to living in small nuclear families, in couples or alone. In a lot of places, the time when it would have been usual to live close to many members of the extended family has now gone. In the area of Liverpool to which I recently moved, however, extended families are more in evidence, but I believe that this can also bring some hindrances to hospitality, which we'll consider later.

> What we have to recognize here is that for many there is a clash in thinking—the way we've grown up versus the way in which the Bible teaches us we should be living.

However, living among our wider family is nowadays not the norm and most of us are used to the small and cosy. In Britain we have a saying 'An Englishman's home is his castle'. Does this mean we all live in palatial dwellings? No, it means that many of us are guilty of pulling up the drawbridge to protect our space. We feel that to invite strangers in is an invasion of our privacy. We can't imagine feeling comfortable with those whom we don't already know well. Perhaps, like me, your only experiences of hospitality as you were growing up were the occasional visits of relations. In my family home it was the annual visits of a couple of aunts, uncles and associated cousins for the traditional salad evening meal followed by trifle. I can remember only one occasion when someone from outside the family came and this caused great consternation as to how they should be fed. This worry was compounded following the visit, because the guests hadn't eaten as much as had been expected! Even now I can remember the feelings of anxiety that surrounded that visit. What we have to recognize here is that for many there is a clash in thinking—the way we've grown up versus the way in which the Bible teaches us we should be living. Whenever there is such a clash, our thinking and our behaviour need to be changed and conformed to biblical standards. The attitudes we have absorbed from our upbringing and conditioning need to be adjusted so that they are pleasing to the Lord whom we serve. This is very much a practical application of the words of Romans 12:2: 'Be transformed by the renewing of your mind.'

I mentioned earlier that those who have the privilege of living among extended families may find a different problem with hospitality. This is that large families can be happily self-contained; they experience a sense of community among themselves and this can lead to neglect of those in the church family who would be encouraged through the ministry of hospitality. So, whether we're living as individuals, or as family units, large or small, we all need to be aware that hospitality is a biblical way of life we should be seeking to practise.

The hurdle here is that, sadly, for many the experience of hospitality is very limited. It hasn't been modelled to them, or, if it has, it's been modelled only at such a high standard that others feel they couldn't possibly do it like that.

A LEARN-AND-PASS-IT-ON MINISTRY— BUT HAVE WE LEARNT IT?

The hurdle here is that, sadly, for many the experience of hospitality is very limited. It hasn't been modelled to them, or, if it has, it's been modelled only at such a high standard that others feel they couldn't possibly do it like that. Perhaps we need to relearn so that we can pass on a biblical example.

We also need to be thankful for those who have given us such an example to follow. As a new Christian in a student setting, I was so encouraged by a family in the church I attended. Jean and Ian regularly invited me into their home, initially for meals with a group of other students. As time went on and our relationship developed, they encouraged me so much in my young faith, talked through issues and helped me to understand and apply God's word to my life. Their sons helped mend my bike and they were even brave enough to lend me their car! I remember that the borrowed car was to be used to ferry students from one city to another! Their Christlike reaction when I returned it with the reversing light stuck on permanently spoke volumes to me as a young Christian. This was my first experience of Christian hospitality.

Then, on returning to my home town, again two couples in the church there opened their homes to me and other young people. Karen and Geoff would regularly provide a Friday supper, but it was the fellowship with them and other Christians that was so important, the opportunity to discuss spiritual issues and to have fun together.

Hilary and Rob had an open house for us young people. Here, those of us not from a Christian home saw what it is to live as a Christian family. A friend puts it like this: 'For a young person from a non-Christian family, time with other Christians can be real respite care.'

Later, on moving to a new city it was Joan, an older single woman who modelled hospitality to me. She had prayed before attending church for wisdom as to whom to invite back for lunch. I was new and so was invited. This was the beginning of a relationship of praying together, which was a vital support to me as a single person in Christian work seeking the Lord's will for my future life and ministry. It was very much a demonstration of Titus 2:4-5: spiritual mothering in action.

I am so thankful to each of these people and to many others who have given me the example of hospitality and the experience of being a part of God's family. For those who haven't grown up in Christian homes, seeing examples of them and of Christian family life is vital in learning how to run a household and parent children in a godly way. I'm sure we can apply the principle of spreading the gospel that is spoken of in 1 Thessalonians 1:6-7 to this situation: 'You became imitators of us … And so you became a model to all the believers'.

Take a moment just to stop and remember any who have served and encouraged you in this way and give thanks to God for them.

LIVING IN AN ENTERTAINMENT SOCIETY

For many, the idea behind inviting others into their homes is to entertain. Maybe we even want to make a good impression on someone else or perhaps further our career prospects. If we're honest it can be a subtle way of showing off, whether that's our magazine-look home or our culinary skills. If this is our motivation, then the food we produce and how we present it become the most important things. We're actually motivated by seeking to satisfy something in ourselves rather than helping to satisfy the needs of others. Again, this is where Bible-teaching clashes with our culture. We need our thinking and actions to be changed so that any hospitality is carried out not from a proud heart, but from a servant heart. If worrying about what people will think about our homes or our cooking stops us from practising hospitality, then we need to re-examine our motives for inviting people in.

> **We're actually motivated by seeking to satisfy something in ourselves rather than helping to satisfy the needs of others... this is where Bible-teaching clashes with our culture.**

I deliberately use the word 'hospitality' as opposed to 'entertaining' when talking about this subject. Both words are used in the Bible; for example we read in Romans 12:13: 'Practise hospitality' and in Hebrews 13:2: 'Do not forget to entertain strangers'. Both 'hospitality' and 'entertain' come from the same Greek word, 'Philoxenia', which means 'love of strangers'. But often today we would understand two very different emphases from these words.

To 'entertain' could be defined as 'provide amusement' or 'give a public performance'. This is the kind of occasion when the boss is invited so that a good impression will be made, perhaps to further career prospects. Or perhaps it's inviting the neighbours in so that they'll be impressed with our DIY skills.

On the other hand, 'hospitality' can be defined as 'the friendly and generous reception of guests'. As the American writer Karen Mains says, 'Entertaining subtly declares —this is mine, these rooms, these adornments, look and admire. Hospitality whispers—what is mine is yours' ('Open heart, open home', Pickering & Inglis 1981). So, as Christians, I believe it is better to use the word 'hospitality'. This helps us to be clear about what it is we are, and are not, about. Hospitality should have nothing to do with pride, with impressing people or looking for a return invitation. But, because we are human, and therefore sinful, we need to guard against this and examine our motives

> **Hospitality should have nothing to do with pride, with impressing people or looking for a return invitation.**

in what we do and how we do it. The decorating may not be completed, the house may not be pristine, the kids may not be perfect, the food may not be cordon bleu; but these things should be no barriers to us sharing our homes with one another. Inviting people into our homes will take effort, but I believe that, as a general rule, the food we provide should reflect what we would normally be cooking. If we'd normally have a roast dinner on Sunday, that's what the guests will have; if it's pasta mid-week, then that's appropriate. We probably will at times want to put in a little more thought and effort—but we need to examine our motives in this. Will our guests feel welcome and appreciated, or are we merely trying to impress them? Pride is such an easy pitfall. I remember a few years ago, when guests were expected, quickly getting the spray polish out and concentrating on the large coffee table in the centre of the room. My thinking was that if this looked good, it would give the impression that everything else was also clean and shiny. As it was a table that showed fingerprints all too easily, I warned my young children to keep their fingers away from it. So, as our guests walked into the room, my young daughter announced, 'Don't touch the table—Mum's just dusted it!' This certainly served as a useful tempering of my pride! However, I have heard some people say that, if it wasn't for guests having been invited, the clearing up and cleaning would never get done; perhaps hospitality in that case is a necessary prompt to housekeeping!

Perhaps it's better to use the example of an unexpected caller: if the home isn't as we might think it ought to be, does that stop us inviting the caller in? If it does, then perhaps we have a pride problem that needs addressing. I can't remember the number of times people have apologized for their home being in a mess; I'm never quite sure how to respond to such a comment. Perhaps I should say, 'Oh dear, so it is. I'll come back when you've cleared it up!' But my intention wasn't to check on housekeeping! So, tidy up if you want to, but don't let untidiness be a barrier to hospitality.

Hospitality is for everyone
An optional extra?

Is hospitality really something in which all of us should be involved? We'll look at some verses from Romans 12 which will help us to answer that question. But before we look at the specific verse that mentions hospitality, it's good to see it in some context, and I believe that the key text when considering this passage is verse 2: 'Do not conform any longer to the pattern of this world, but be transformed by the renewing of your mind.'

> **'Do not conform any longer to the pattern of this world, but be transformed by the renewing of your mind.'**

Our thinking is to be transformed. In the last chapter we were thinking about hurdles to hospitality. Remember that we called them hurdles, not barriers. Here in verse 2 we see that as Christians, as citizens primarily of God's society, our thinking is to be changed. Then, as a result of our renewed thinking, our actions are also to be changed. There may be natural or cultural hurdles, but as we seek to live to please God, we should be seeking to leap over these hurdles. It's easy to see that any kind of leaping takes effort—especially at first! But on watching experienced hurdlers, it can be seen that, with practice, the action becomes natural and a pleasure to watch.

The following excerpts from Romans 12:9-13 can help as we attempt to leap those hurdles: 'Love must be sincere … be devoted to one another … honour one another … never be lacking in zeal … be joyful in hope, patient in affliction, faithful in prayer. Share with God's people who are in need. Practise hospitality.'

These verses are a help in focusing our thinking on how we are to live out the life of love to which we're called. If we each live like this, the fellowship of the church will be greatly enriched. Looking at these verses, I don't imagine any of us would disagree that this is how we should be living. Yet we may seek to embrace this passage and still manage to forget the last couple of words—the command to 'practise hospitality'. We wouldn't ever consider loving, honouring or serving optional, but somehow we feel that practising hospitality is something we can choose to do or not. When we read all of this chapter, we would have to agree that *all* the commands here are applicable to *all* Christians so therefore we must also conclude that hospitality is for all, too.

Hospitality is not an optional extra in the Christian life, but is something we need to get to grips with, for two reasons: firstly, for the good of our own spiritual growth and service as we are obedient to our Lord; secondly, for the strengthening of our local church fellowship.

ANGELS TOO?

In Hebrews 13:2 we read: 'Do not forget to entertain strangers, for by so doing some people have entertained angels without knowing it.'

> **When did you or I last give hospitality to angels? Perhaps we need to consider that the verse says that it could happen as we 'entertain strangers'.**

When did you or I last give hospitality to angels? Perhaps we need to consider that the verse says that it could happen as we 'entertain strangers'. An easy trap to fall into is to invite into our homes only those we like, those with whom we feel comfortable or have much in common. It's good to have our friends visit our homes, but we need to welcome others in, too. When thinking of strangers in the church, perhaps we could think of those who are new, those on the fringe, or even those who might seem a little strange! So often we will find that, as we welcome such people into our homes, our eyes are opened to appreciate them, and our lives are enriched too.

It's worth thinking about the purpose of angels. Knowledgeable books tell me that the word 'angel' comes from a Greek word that means 'to deliver a message'. So angels are messengers of God. This is very obvious in the case of Abraham and Sarah in Genesis 18. They gave hospitality to three visitors and these visitors had a message for them from God about a little bundle of great joy who'd be putting in an appearance in a year's time. These visitors also told Abraham about God's coming judgement on Sodom. Perhaps we need to be open to the possibility of God speaking to us through our visitors. It may be that in their conversation God will reveal or confirm something of his plans and purposes for us. So don't miss the angels! We may never know how our hospitality might count in God's scheme of things.

ROOM ON THE ROOF!

One day Elisha went to Shunem. And a well-to-do woman was there, who urged him to stay for a meal. So whenever he came by, he stopped there to eat. She said to her husband, "I know that this man who often comes our way is a holy man of God. Let's make a small room on the roof and put in it a bed and a table, a chair and a lamp for him. Then he can stay there whenever he comes to us"
(2 Kings 4:8-10).

Here we meet 'Mr and Mrs Shunem'. There's just the two of them in the family. They respond to a need that they see. It's the wife who urges Elisha to come and have his dinner when he's passing that way. It was probably as they were chatting over a meal that another need was recognized. Elisha, this travelling preacher, could do with somewhere to stay. So Mrs Shunem, obviously the more sensitive of the two, goes on to urge her husband to see the need. I wonder how the division of labour worked out for the practicalities; was it Mr Shunem building the extension and Mrs Shunem doing the interior design, or the other way round? Both man and wife are involved in providing this hospitality.

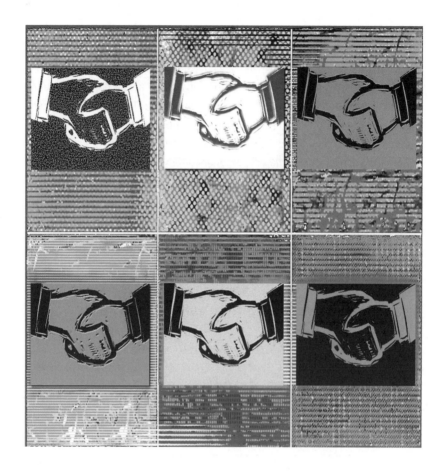

For three years I worked with students and stayed in many different places, some of which were welcoming and comfortable, while others were not. I remember the floor that smelt of damp and had silverfish darting about, and also the room that I shared with the baby of the household! Having had no experience of babies I spent half the night worrying that he'd wake and I'd have to work out what to do with him. But I don't think anything surpasses the experience of a colleague of mine who had gone to help out with an evangelistic mission. A student had kindly moved out of his room for her, but omitted to think about getting clean sheets—those on the bed looked as if they'd been there for at least the whole term, if not the previous one too! I can imagine how good it would have been for Elisha to have had this space he could call his own. Perhaps you have a home with a room you could ask the Lord to use. I think of Terri and Pete who thought in this way. After their children had left home, they equipped one spare room with a double bed and the other with twin beds. I'm sure they've found that, in giving hospitality, they often receive so much more than they give. It would have been the same for Mr and Mrs Shunem. Elisha is so encouraged by this practical service that he wants to bless them, too: 'You have gone to all this trouble for us. Now what can be done for you?' (verse 13).

With the help of his servant, Elisha discovers that they are a childless couple, and so God gives them the promise through him that they will have a son. Understandably, given the husband's age, they were speechless! But, a year later, these words were proved true as they held their son. Perhaps this isn't the way for all of us to practise hospitality, but it could be for some.

AFTER A MEETING

Jesus left the synagogue and went to the home of Simon. Now Simon's mother-in-law was suffering from a high fever, and they asked Jesus to help her. So he bent over her and rebuked the fever, and it left her. She got up at once and began to wait on them (Luke 4:38-39).

Perhaps this is an example to which more of us can relate in offering hospitality. Jesus has been having a busy time. He's been teaching, healing, and dealing with both men's opposition and evil spirits. Simon invites Jesus back home after a meeting. I'm sure this welcome into a home was appreciated by Jesus in this time of busyness and pressure. Here again we see that the host receives. Jesus heals Simon's mother-in law and she is then able to help serve the guests. Perhaps it meant that all the washing-up wasn't left for Simon after everyone had gone!

For us this could be something pre-arranged or organized on the spur of the moment, but whichever it is, it's an opportunity for some simple hospitality. Perhaps we could invite people to join us after a church meeting, or even before. Maybe we could invite someone who would enjoy sharing the family meal before a mid-week meeting. It's good to be looking out for a variety of opportunities, both planned and spontaneous, to get on with the practice of hospitality.

ONLY FOR THE MATURE?

When she [Lydia] and the members of her household were baptized, she invited us to her home. "If you consider me a believer in the Lord," she said, "come and stay at my house." And she persuaded us (Acts 16:15).

Lydia is a recent convert, and following her baptism she invites Paul and Silas to her home. From this we see that hospitality is a natural outworking of faith, not something that only mature Christians can engage in. The first people to show me hospitality were gracious enough to accept an invitation to my student accommodation and suffer my limited culinary skills; I remember the recipe I used on that occasion—I found it on the chilli powder jar! Student ministry gave me the opportunity to be on the receiving end of such first steps. Stir-fried vegetables with cheese sauce, and toasted sandwiches with custard stand out, not forgetting spaghetti bolognese five days in a row!

There's no need to wait until you've been a Christian for a long time; invite older Christians into your home and you'll be an encouragement to them as, no doubt, they will be to you. There's also no need to wait until your culinary skills are matured either; keep it simple, within your capabilities, or stick to boiling the kettle. In books on entertaining we read that a recipe should always be tried out first before giving it to guests. As this is hospitality, I don't believe that rule applies. A memory that stands out is of a first attempt with tofu; I

confess that the hosts spat it out, while our friend swallowed a whole cube. Not a meal to be remembered for its flavour but for its fun. Or our friend's dessert that wouldn't set, the pause between courses getting longer and longer as he kept checking it; but a runny dessert with friends is better than the perfect dessert eaten alone. In fact it's often the case that when things go wrong and are responded to in a light-hearted way, a greater bond is formed.

A MUST FOR LEADERS

Now the overseer must be above reproach, the husband of but one wife, temperate, self-controlled, respectable, hospitable, able to teach, not given to drunkenness, not violent but gentle, not quarrelsome, not a lover of money (1 Timothy 3:2-3).

These verses will often be used as a checklist when looking at potential leaders and 'hospitable' is there in the middle. As in every area of the Christian life, leaders should set an example. If an example is set, it's not so that people can look and say, 'Aren't they living godly lives!', but it's to encourage others by that example. Leaders are usually busy people, but if the importance of hospitality is recognized, coupled with a desire to be obedient, then time will be made to invite others in. Relaxed time together in an unhurried situation, without a pastoral agenda, can only serve to help. Leaders will deepen and strengthen relationships with those they lead. They will become more approachable. There will be a development of mutual understanding, love and respect.

BUT I'M ON MY OWN

No widow may be put on the list of widows unless she is over sixty, has been faithful to her husband, and is well known for her good deeds, such as bringing up children, showing hospitality, washing the feet of the saints, helping those in trouble and devoting herself to all kinds of good deeds (1 Timothy 5:9-10).

These words seem at first to be quite harsh. For a widow to be able to receive support from the church, these things were expected of her. Widows were supposed to be practising hospitality as well as doing other good deeds. I believe these principles can be applied to any who are on their own, whether widowed or single for any other reason. I've already mentioned Joan, a lady on her own, who encouraged me so much through opening her home to me and so building a relationship. Remember Titus 2:4: 'Then they can train the younger women'. We see here the example that an older woman is to set to a younger woman—age and marital status are rarely barriers.

My culinary skills took some time to develop. As a single woman I would share giving hospitality with a friend who was a doctor at the local hospital. We would use her flat as she would often be 'on call'. She was happy to do the cooking, while I found that the small talk came naturally. So we used our different giftings to complement each other and we practised together.

Remember, any giving of hospitality can be tailored to your own abilities and means. Don't forget, breaking open a packet of biscuits is just as much hospitality as is offering a full roast dinner or an exotic meal.

27

What hospitality looks like

HOSPITALITY IS ABOUT SERVANTHOOD

Different areas of church life bring opportunities to develop our Christlikeness in different ways. Hospitality gives us the opportunity to develop our service of one another. We've already considered the necessity of the practice of hospitality for leaders. In this context we need to consider the words of Jesus: 'If anyone wants to be first, he must be the very last, and the servant of all' (Mark 9:35); and 'whoever wants to become great among you must be your servant' (Mark 10:43). It's about having the same sort of attitude as Jesus, who 'did not come to be served, but to serve' (Matthew 20:28).

When I worked with students a number of years ago, it was often easy to spot potential leaders, not so much by their gifting and charisma, but by their willingness to serve. The person who would quietly get on with washing up the coffee cups, or take a lead in putting the chairs away, would often be the one who would make a good leader. This attitude of service shouldn't end just because someone has a leadership position. In our church, one of the elders was always willing to be involved in the practical work as need arose. He'd be found getting on with sweeping up the glass from a broken window, or sorting out a blocked toilet. Perhaps those things should primarily be the work of a deacon, but no position of leadership should be a bar to being willing to serve.

> **Hospitality is a servant ministry for each of us, whatever our position or calling.**

Hospitality is a servant ministry for each of us, whatever our position or calling. These verses can help us again at this point: 'No widow may be put on the list of widows unless she is over sixty, has been faithful to her husband, and is well known for her good deeds, such as bringing up children, showing hospitality,

washing the feet of the saints, helping those in trouble and devoting herself to all kinds of good deeds' (1 Timothy 5:9-10).

This widow is expected to practise good deeds if she is to qualify for help. Her good deeds are to include bringing up her children; that means recognizing that any children she has are a gift from God, and taking this responsibility seriously. I find it encouraging to have mothering highlighted here as an honoured and worthwhile task.

If hospitality is new and a bit daunting, start practising with those whom you think you'll find easier, and work towards those whom you imagine to be harder

This widow is also to be getting on with foot-washing. In those days, when living in a dusty area and wearing open-toed footwear were the norm, this was a necessary service and would have been appreciated by those with tired and dirty feet. That's obviously not so necessary for us today, especially as it's often so easy to take a quick shower. But perhaps we can look out for other ways in which we can give practical help. I am indebted to those who week after week took away my basket of crumpled clothes and returned them beautifully ironed, because I had a shoulder problem.

Timothy also instructs widows to help those in trouble and to be devoted to other good deeds that would have taken him too long to list. Hospitality is included here. The picture is very much of someone willing to serve others, look out for the needs of others and do all that is in her power to help meet those needs.

Hospitality is about spending time with those with whom we find it less easy to get on. We often remember to invite home those who are new to the church, and this is obviously good in helping them to settle in or perhaps even to decide if your church fellowship is right for them. But we also need to look around the church for those with whom we've never really communicated, those about whom we know little, those who seem to be on the edge. So often when we spend time with these people, we find that we enjoy a fellowship we'd never have imagined, and that our lives are enriched and our hearts encouraged. If hospitality is new and a bit daunting, start practising with those whom you think you'll find easier, and work towards those whom you imagine to be harder—though as I've indicated, you'll often be pleasantly surprised.

HOSPITALITY IS NOT WITHOUT COST

It's interesting to read these words in 1 Peter 4:9: 'Offer hospitality to one another without grumbling.' We may find it surprising to read that grumbling can be linked to giving hospitality. But as it's mentioned, there must be a reason for it. As this letter is addressed to a scattered group of Christians, it would seem that grumbling wasn't just a problem for one particular group in one area. So why might giving hospitality lead to grumbling? I think it is because of the cost involved. By 'cost' I don't mean the money you pay for the food. but rather the cost in time and effort, and even on your home.

When hospitality takes place, there is always a cost in terms of time, the time we spend together. There may also be a cost in preparation time—working out what food, if any, will be appropriate, shopping for it and preparing it. This obviously involves a cost in effort, too, not to mention money.

Another cost you might discover is that people don't always behave in the ways in which you'd expect them to. When a meal is involved, sometimes adults as well as children can be hard work because of what they will or won't eat. Sometimes you may find that even when you'd checked that a certain food would be all right with them, they don't like it. It could be that you've bought a different brand from the one they like, or cooked the food slightly differently from the way they'd do it. Sometimes the meal you've worked hard on is liberally covered in ketchup! Perhaps this all helps to keep any pride in check!

Sometimes the meal you've worked hard on is liberally covered in ketchup! Perhaps this all helps to keep any pride in check!

We might also be tempted to grumble because our guests allow their children to do whatever they want, while ours are trained to stay at the table, sitting in seats while everyone eats. My children gradually learned that when visitors did something which they weren't allowed to do, it wasn't up to them to correct it!

Sometimes, even though we know this is a servant ministry, we can feel hurt if we receive no thanks.

Sometimes, even though we know this is a servant ministry, we can feel hurt if we receive no thanks. Again, rather than grumble, we should be thankful that we have had the opportunity to serve. A number of years ago, a young woman from a very difficult background spent a lot of time in our home. Some who knew her struggled with the fact that however much you did for her, she never said 'thank you'. But, as time went on, the continued love and giving had an effect on her and she opened up, emotionally and spiritually. That first 'thanks' was so precious, not because it made us feel appreciated, but because we recognized that she was learning skills that would actually make it easier for others to accept her.

Another part of the cost could be the damage that is done to your possessions: a damp cup placed on a polished table, a buckle on the furniture, or mud on the floor, for example. One memorable experience of ours is of a leaky nappy on the carpet! All of these things challenge our loving spirit, our forgiveness, our Christlikeness. When we used to host the young people's group at one time, a rather ebullient young girl would, in her high-spirited clumsiness, manage to break a glass most weeks. It became something of a joke, but we were delighted when Christmas came. We received from her a box of glasses, and we were touched that she had even taken the time to find a matching set!

Sometimes giving one-off hospitality can lead to much more. A young woman once came into our home for a meal, and that developed into her spending weekends and an evening a week with us, as well as us supporting her through an unplanned pregnancy. One family invited a man for Christmas dinner; he stayed for thirty-five years, and the family eventually even arranged his funeral!

So hospitality involves costs which can be a challenge, but rather than grumble, we should be thankful.

HOSPITALITY NEEDS PRACTICE!

'Share with God's people who are in need. Practise hospitality' (Romans 12:13). This verse instructs us to 'practise hospitality'. Perhaps this simply means 'get on and do it', but I tend to think that with hospitality there is also a need to practise so that we'll get better. Again, I don't mean 'better' so that visitors will be really impressed, but rather so that we can do it more easily and more often. Better, so that our focus becomes more on encouraging our guests and sharing fellowship with them.

We thought earlier that for many, hospitality hasn't always been a natural part of life; therefore it needs practice so that it does become a more instinctive part of our renewed, redeemed lives. Some do seem to have a particular gift of hospitality, but for the many for whom this isn't the case, we do need to practise. Some find it easy to chat to people whom they don't know so well; others find this more difficult. Again, practice will help develop this skill.

Some do seem to have a particular gift of hospitality, but for the many for whom this isn't the case, we do need to practise.

If we have a desire to grow in holiness, to serve the Lord as he desires, we can't ignore this command. As we are obedient, as we do practise, we will find that it does get easier and then we'll find that our desire to serve in this way will grow.

Getting ready for hospitality

WHEN IT'S MORE THAN A BISCUIT

If a meal is to form some part of the hospitality you're planning, it's good to give it some concentrated thought before the event. This will then allow time to spend with people rather than pans. It's probably just a matter of personal choice as to whether you are happy to have people in the kitchen with you while you're preparing a meal. It can be good, as this unfocused attention can help people to relax. However, personally, I find that if it's more than just a bit of finishing-off that's required, it's hard to give adequate attention to both food and guests. We know ourselves and need to decide what works best for us. I prefer to do as much preparation as possible before people arrive. The following explains how I work this out practically.

If hospitality is to follow the Sunday morning service, I aim to start my preparation on Saturday. This may mean preparing some of the vegetables; perhaps this is not quite as good nutritionally as preparing them on Sunday, but it's a price I'm willing to pay. There's a choice to be made over dessert. If it's frozen and needs defrosting, it needs to be taken out of the freezer! If I can plan it in, a cold dessert can often be prepared in advance, while if the weather is cold I might prepare a crumble topping the day before, or buy it in a packet.

We mustn't forget that the Sabbath, our Sunday, was designed by God both for gathering together for worship and for rest. You may decide on a cold meal that can be almost fully prepared the day before. Any advance preparation you do will help the day feel less like a day of manual labour. Whatever day of the week you choose to have guests, a bit of forward planning helps hospitality to run smoothly so that you can concentrate on the guests.

The choices we make about food affect the 'people' part of our hospitality, and that means it's often best to make simple choices. There's nothing wrong with sharing a takeaway with guests, though it might be worth checking first

We mustn't forget that the Sabbath, our Sunday, was designed by God both for gathering together for worship and for rest. Any advance preparation you do will help the day feel less like a day of manual labour.

that they like hot curries or whatever it is you'd choose. Many supermarkets also sell really good prepared meals, desserts and cakes, many at a reasonable price.

A number of years ago, a couple wanted to invite my husband and I for an evening meal. They had a large young family and a busy household. They didn't let this hinder their hospitality, but instead we enjoyed a meal together from the supermarket chilled cabinet. But, more importantly, it began both a relationship which enabled us to work together in the church and a lasting friendship.

As you practise hospitality you will learn to do things that will help keep it simple. For instance, if you came to our house on a Sunday, we would most probably eat a simple roast dinner at midday. We've now developed a vegetarian alternative, too. If you stayed until the evening, we would then eat such things as toasted teacakes, followed by cake in the winter, sandwiches and cake in the summer. Having a 'formula' for meals makes shopping, preparation, and life generally, much simpler!

If Sunday hospitality means that you get to church late or hassled, or even miss it altogether, then priorities need sorting out and Sunday hospitality probably isn't for you. Personally, I've found that if I leave my devotional time until I've finished getting the meal ready, it never happens, but if I put it in first, I still manage to get enough done.

I'm not saying that it's never right to serve a more elaborate meal. If it's possible for this to be prepared in advance, that can be good. But I do believe it's right to question our motives—are we out to impress or to bless? I can think of one occasion recently when we'd taken perhaps a bit more trouble than usual. It was to be for an evening meal. We had the time and both of us fancied cooking something a bit different, sharing main course and dessert between us. Our visitors were delayed by a sudden family crisis. They arrived understandably frayed and stressed. We enjoyed the meal together and relaxed in one another's company. Sometimes the provision of food is

important and can be a great encouragement in itself. It's a bit like when Elijah was feeling very down in 1 Kings 19: '"I have had enough, LORD," he said "Take my life"' (verse 4).

What did God do? Give him an amazing spiritual experience? No, he gave him the gift of rest and food—twice! 'An angel touched him and said, "Get up and eat."' (verse 5). Only after these physical needs had been taken care of was he able to cope with the spiritual experience God had for him. Perhaps sometimes we are to be like that angelic messenger to Elijah, showing God's care to a battered Christian.

PEOPLE

While a formula for meals can be useful at certain times, flexibility is needed as to when to invite different people, and for what. Sometimes elderly people seem to appreciate a tea: that's often long enough for them if there's a boisterous family in your home. Younger people might prefer supper after a service. For others an evening meal or a summer barbecue works well. We need to consider what the best time would be for us and for our guests.

Be specific. When you invite people, let them know what to expect. I don't mean that you need to go through the menu, but do be specific as to what exactly they are invited for, e.g., 'Come for dinner'; 'Come for dinner and tea'; 'Come for tea'. However, if I say 'Come for dinner' on Sunday, I always make sure I have something ready in case this naturally develops into tea as well. The word 'supper' can mean anything from a drink and biscuit to a three-course meal, so do give some indication of what to expect.

I remember one occasion when I'd been invited 'for the evening'. I was late in from work, so grabbed a large sandwich and dashed round. I then discovered that 'the evening' included a substantial dinner. I struggled manfully through as much of it as I could!

YOURSELF

Hospitality is a practical ministry, but it is spiritual, too. It's good to pray both about whom to invite and, when the invitation has been given, that the time will be useful, that people will feel at ease, that fellowship will be enjoyed and relationships strengthened. Having learned from Joan's example many years ago, I frequently pray not only about whom to invite, but also for wisdom in conversation. We need to ensure that both our motivation and aim in hospitality are right. Then we're less likely to fall into the traps of either grumbling or just going through the motions.

> **Hospitality is a practical ministry, but it is spiritual, too. It's good to pray both about whom to invite**

I can remember many occasions of such prayer being answered, but perhaps one that stands out most is with a couple we'd got to know in hospital when the wife and I met on the post-natal ward. We felt that the husband was showing some spiritual interest, and on that evening in our home, as he insisted on helping my husband with the washing-up, he told him he was a backslidden Christian.

In hospitality we are seeking to get to know people better and so we also want to develop spiritual relationships with them. We need to guide the conversation so that it isn't only trivial chatter but moves onto spiritual issues. Perhaps this could be done by talking about how some recent teaching or personal reading has helped you. Or, if you know that the guests are Christians, ask them how they came to know the Lord. If they're not Christians, pray both for the opportunity and the boldness to share something of your own testimony and your walk with the Lord.

> **In hospitality we are seeking to get to know people better and so we also want to develop spiritual relationships with them.**

THE WHOLE FAMILY

Many men are great cooks, but they are often too happy just to let the woman get on with it. If you're married, don't always assume it's the wife's job to do the cooking. In our household we both get involved when possible, as other commitments allow. Sometimes one of us will prepare the main course, while the other does the dessert, or one does the preparation and the other the finishing-off. But, whether they are doing the cooking or not, all family members should be encouraged to take part in welcoming others into our homes.

If you have children who would enjoy helping with food preparation, let them do so, even if their results might not be quite as professional as yours. I remember that when my children were young they would particularly enjoy helping to bake and decorate cakes. I had to tell myself to relax over this; their idea of presentation wasn't always the same as mine, but I recognized that their pleasure at being involved was more important than this. Children can also help in such things as setting the table or fetching extra chairs. Involvement like this is part of training our children so that they will find it

> **Children can be great at helping to put people at ease, but they do need training so that they don't dominate. Conversation should include them, but not revolve only around them.**

natural to practise hospitality in the future, as well as feeling involved now.

Children can be great at helping to put people at ease, but they do need training so that they don't dominate. Conversation should include them, but not revolve only around them. As they grow older, and perhaps especially once they are teenagers, it might be good to expect that they at least stay around for the meal but can then disappear later—unless other teens have been invited, of course. It may be possible to invite friends of our children to join in the hospitality, so encouraging a more positive view of giving hospitality.

Just a note on washing up at this point: be flexible. If people are going to be with you for a large part of the day, you might decide that chatting over the washing-up is fine as part of this. But when time is more limited, we tend to leave it until later.

BE CREATIVE AND FLEXIBLE

At times it's worth thinking carefully about how to make the occasion fit the guests. Kathy and Leo and their two girls were from the United States and were living in England for a year. Members of the church were being very good at offering hospitality; however, when chatting with Kathy, I discovered that, although they were grateful for this, they were finding it a bit hard. It seemed that most of their hosts had decided to give them that traditional British favourite, roast beef and Yorkshire pudding. As this was definitely not popular with their girls it was becoming difficult for the parents! So I rang an American friend of mine and asked for advice on what she thought they'd appreciate. The meal she suggested was very much enjoyed, especially by the parents who didn't have to battle with the girls over it. My friend had given instructions on how to make iced tea; the family were particularly pleased with this as I'd made it from scratch whereas they always used the instant variety!

On another occasion we had three young couples round to our house. One of the men, recently engaged, was new to the church and wasn't finding it easy to mix. As the others were recently married, we asked them to bring their wedding albums. Establishing a common point of interest really helped the conversation flow, not to mention the laughs over our somewhat older wedding album!

Another time we'd also invited three couples round: one couple were Christians, but the other two wives had non-Christian husbands. Recognizing that these two men might not feel so much at their ease, we planned a 'games and pizza' evening. We had a Trivial Pursuit board in the centre of the table and we ate pizza around it, playing the game at the same time. This seemed to really relax these men; there was lots of fun as well as a building of relationships.

It can be good to invite guests with a common interest. But it's also good to mix and match a bit.

But perhaps your creativity doesn't have to be so extreme. You might, for example, want to invite those with young children but your home would make it very restricted for them. Invite them when the weather is likely to be good and plan in a walk to the local park or somewhere similar. There will then be good opportunities for conversation as you walk and as the children play.

It can be good to invite guests with a common interest. But it's also good to mix and match a bit. Older people may well enjoy the opportunity to get to know a young family; or someone who lives alone may well appreciate the noise and bustle of a larger gathering. Just to be included can be incredibly valuable for someone struggling with loneliness.

Tools of hospitality

YOUR HOME

We've seen that hospitality isn't about showing off our homes and so neither the size nor state of our homes should be a bar to our offering hospitality. If we're worried about what people will think about the way we live, then we've missed the point. All that's needed is a willingness for our homes to be used.

PROPS

There are some things in our homes that can make giving hospitality easier both for us and our guests. Having some easy to read, coffee-table books lying around can be useful, especially if you're on your own. Then, if you need to go to check on the oven, it gives guests something relaxing to flick through.

In our sitting room we have gradually built up a selection of small puzzles, the wooden fit-together type or similar. We have found these particularly useful with teens, who have a tendency to feel awkward in new situations. We tell them to have a go, and often chatter develops over the possible solution.

As my children grew older I kept a small box of chunky building bricks. This included a small train track and a few figures and animals. These are both safe and fun for a wide age range. My children are very good at helping with the building, which helps put younger children at their ease. If you don't have any toys at home, see what you can find at a jumble sale, or ask parents to bring toys with them. For very young children you'll also need to check that the parents can bring a high chair or toddler seat. Will the food you're preparing be suitable, or will they bring baby food? Depending on the length and timing of the visit, a suitable place in which a young child can sleep might also need to be provided.

RECIPES

If cooking isn't your greatest delight, ask friends for easy recipes. My husband has a theory: 'If you can read [and it appears you can], you can cook.' A tip: read through the whole recipe first before starting any preparation or cooking. Libraries also have recipe books. Don't be too ambitious at first; build your confidence and then extend your repertoire. If, when you yourself are receiving hospitality, you are enjoying the food, ask your host for the recipe; often things aren't as difficult as you might imagine. Asking for a recipe will also be a great encouragement to your host!

Sensitivity in hospitality

AN OPEN DOOR?

Some people practise an 'open door' type of hospitality. This is where others know that they can call in at any time and join in with whatever the family is doing. It tends to be couples or families who engage in this type of ministry, as it's very difficult to practise it if you are a single person. It would usually be inappropriate for a single person to give hospitality to a member of the opposite sex, or even to lone younger individuals of the same sex. Sadly, there is an ever-increasing need to be careful so as to give no 'appearance of evil' (1 Thessalonians 5:22. AV).

> **Some of us find that, while we love to be with and serve others much of the time, we also need time to get on with work at home.**

But some are able to offer this 'open door' and it can be a great help and encouragement for many. However, it isn't appropriate for all. Some of us find that, while we love to be with and serve others much of the time, we also need time to get on with work at home. This is particularly so for those whose workplace is the home. It's also important that family relationships don't suffer if we are practising this 'open door' kind of ministry.

CHILDREN

Young children often enjoy the company of others, but there is a need to give teenagers in particular time and space. I remember a young girl, whose parents had an 'open door'. She felt that there was never any privacy: 'If I want to talk to my mum we have to sit in the dark so people don't know we're in!' This built great resentment in her towards the church and Christian service.

Instead, I would encourage parents with children of any age to welcome your

children's friends into your home. There are good reasons for this. It's good for children from non-Christian homes to experience a Christian home. A young girl had visited our home a number of times and one day, as the children were about to eat, I asked who would like to say grace. To my surprise, this girl said that she would. It was very special to hear this little girl say a simple prayer of thanks to God. She had been listening and learning.

I also believe that, if you have your children's friends in your home when they are young, this practice is more likely to continue as they get older. As parents we need to keep the lines of communication open, and children who are used to having their friends welcomed into their homes are more likely to talk about their friends.

If discipline of our children is necessary when visitors are there, this should be carried out in normal ways.

Are we living consistent lives in front of our children? Are we usually fire and thunder behind closed doors, but sweetness and light when visitors are there? Our children will see this inconsistency and it will harm the example we are trying to set. A challenge for us as parents would be to think whether we'd be happy for a visitor to see how we're behaving—remembering that there is one who always sees. If discipline of our children is necessary when visitors are there, this should be carried out in normal ways. Occasionally, in extreme situations, we may choose to ask our child to leave the room with us and then deal with the misdemeanour. Perfection is not required, but an aim towards consistency is. I confess to having been envious of friends who are able to speak in another language to their children without the guests knowing what is being said. But perhaps doing this isn't good manners anyway!

We also need to be careful that our children do not see us making an effort only for visitors and never for them. Mary K. Mohler illustrates this; her daughter once asked her about the chocolate cake she was preparing: 'Is that for people, or for us?' (from 'Devotions for ministry wives', edited by Barbara Hughes, Zondervan 2002).

If the plan is for your children not to eat with you and the guests, make sure that the children don't feel that they will be missing out.

If the plan is for your children not to eat with you and the guests, make sure that the children don't feel that they will be missing out. Sometimes giving them a treat they'd enjoy would be a good idea in these circumstances.

Our children may need some guidelines that will help when there are visitors. They need to know that the guests aren't there for the sole purpose of playing with, or talking to, them. Children will sometimes, in seeking to be hospitable, ask the guest to go into their room with them. They need to know that this is only appropriate if the guest is a similar-aged child.

Over the years we have received positive comments about our children in relation to hospitality. It's always good to pass on such comments to the children, as this will both help them to be more positive about having guests and encourage them to continue to behave in acceptable ways.

NON-CHRISTIAN SPOUSE

If you have a partner who is not a Christian, care needs to be exercised. Some non-Christian partners are happy to have Christians in their homes. They view it as being similar to the way they'd invite home their friends from, for example, a sports club. If this is the case, then go ahead. It's obviously good for the non-Christian to mix with Christians and so to build relationships in an environment where he or she won't feel threatened. Just be careful not to overdo it.

If your partner isn't happy with this, you may be able to find other opportunities when you can invite people into your home. Perhaps if you're home on your own at some point in the day, your partner would be happy for you to have church contacts in for coffee or supper at these times.

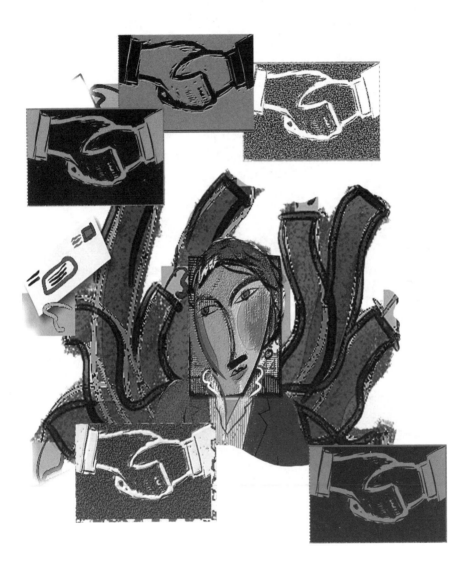

Receiving hospitality

THANKS

What a joy it's been to be on the receiving-end of great sensitivity in hospitality! We've moved house a number of times and have been indebted to those who have provided food for us at these stressful times and relieved us of having to prepare a meal. Thank you to those who have welcomed us in our dusty and grimy state on such occasions!

> **Those of you who for any length of time have had to rely on takeaways or eating out will know how special home-cooking, and fresh vegetables in particular, can be.**

Some other personal examples come from a time following an operation, when pain made daily tasks extremely difficult and, at times, impossible. Those who brought meals to our home were such a help, especially to my husband, who not only had his own responsibilities as a pastor, but had to deal with all the family responsibilities, too. Invitations to eat at others' homes were also appreciated at this time. We are indebted to those who understood that, because of the nature of this physical problem, we had to leave quickly after eating, as rest was needed again.

Another time we were without a kitchen for six weeks, which was no fun, but again there were those who not only fed us but also let us use their washing machines. Those of you who for any length of time have had to rely on takeaways or eating out will know how special home-cooking, and fresh vegetables in particular, can be.

ACCEPT GLADLY

To refuse hospitality can be very damaging to fellowship. If you are invited out and there is no practical reason to stop you going, then accept. Sometimes it can be that those who are good at offering hospitality find it hard to receive. It can also be a problem for those who like to 'keep themselves to themselves'. Again, attitude is important; to refuse is to stop someone else having the opportunity to serve the Lord. To keep to yourself seems to bear no resemblance to Paul's image of the body in 1 Corinthians 12:21: 'The eye cannot say to the hand, "I don't need you!"' Remember: not only accepting hospitality but also realizing a need of hospitality is to give others an opportunity to serve the Lord as they serve us.

EXPECT NOTHING

It's probably natural that if we're invited to someone's home, we look forward to the meal we've been promised. But remember that you're not there for a gourmet meal. So if it isn't what you expected, be gracious.

Those of us with children need to train them to eat what is put in front of them, or, if that's not possible, then at least not to make a fuss. This might be the case for some adults, too! If there's a real problem with a particular food, perhaps a nut allergy or something similar, mention this when you're invited— but this isn't a licence to give a list of your likes and dislikes. The old missionary prayer of 'I'll get it down if you keep it down' can be uttered silently. I remember years ago arriving at a home and being told, 'We're eating mackerel'; as fish is my least favourite food this was a challenge, but with the above prayer and every mouthful of fish masked by the vegetables, it was managed! I remember, too, challenging occasions when working with students; some of their culinary efforts were interesting, to say the least. I've already mentioned the stir-fry that had chunks of corned beef smothered in cheese sauce. It was certainly memorable, as were the toasted sandwiches with custard!

BE PREPARED

Keep in mind that your hosts might not necessarily find it a natural thing to have you in their home, so try to make it as simple as possible for them. A nervous host who keeps checking that things are OK for you needs reassurance, so be willing to give it, but be careful not to overdo it. Be ready to make conversation; remember that you are not there to be entertained, but to learn to function together more effectively as part of the body of Christ. If you are taking children with you it's good to be prepared. Toys or another appropriate activity can be taken. I have a friend who keeps a small tub of toys in the car for such occasions. Some rules can be useful too; such as to stay in the same room unless invited to explore the home further, or not to touch anything unless invited to do so. I remember when one of my children was a toddler and was behaving in too relaxed a way when visiting, so that if hungry or thirsty would ask for something, or if feeling like being subtle, would stare at the biscuit tin. So the instruction was given not to ask. On the next visit, when my child was offered a drink and biscuit, the offer was declined. As this wasn't the response I expected I had to find out why. My child thought that to accept an offer was the same thing as asking—a bit more clarification was needed!

> **If you are taking children with you it's good to be prepared. Toys or another appropriate activity can be taken. I have a friend who keeps a small tub of toys in the car for such occasions.**

Thank you

The last word—rewards of hospitality

I'm not talking here about the bunches of flowers or boxes of chocolates that some may bring. As nice as these things are, I'm not convinced they really are necessary when one part of the church family is hospitable to another. In fact, in some cultures this tradition can be prohibitive to hospitality. Some missionaries in Latvia were keen to have people to their home for a meal. But they found out that Latvians can't visit without coming laden with gifts. This was difficult, as the missionaries recognized that the desire to be generous with gifts would cause a financial problem to those people who lived on very limited means. Latvia abounds with flower stalls which, though beautiful, give evidence of this cultural norm of always taking a gift. A word, or even a note of appreciation, is often more encouraging to the one who has given the hospitality.

We get to know and appreciate those people to whom, perhaps, we wouldn't be drawn naturally.

So what are the real rewards of hospitality? Most importantly they are seen in the strengthening of relationships and so in the building-up of the church. We get to know and appreciate those people to whom, perhaps, we wouldn't be drawn naturally. We find out what motivates them, what concerns and burdens them. We often find out that people are much more interesting to know than we'd ever have realized if we had not spent this time together. The saying 'Don't judge a book by its cover' is apt. Following a move to a new area, our children, like us, were struggling to remember who everyone was. But after a visit to a couple's home they certainly remembered them: 'Oh yes, they're the skydiving, computer expert grandparents!'

As we spend time together, barriers are broken down, and trust and understanding are built up. We see in Acts 2 that fellowship builds up the church: 'All the believers were together and had everything in common. Selling their possessions and goods, they gave to anyone as he had need… Every day they continued to meet together … they broke bread in their homes and ate together … And the Lord added to their number daily those who were being saved' (verses 44-47).

As the Christians cared for one another and spent time together, many others were saved. A community in which its members care for and love one another is attractive to outsiders. Many in our society live lives without any real sense of community; this is something which the church can offer to fragmented families and isolated individuals.

As well as getting to know our guests better, it is also good, when we have a number of people together in our home, to see guests relating to one another and supportive relationships being built up. Where non-Christians are included, preconceptions, which may well be misconceptions, can so often be broken down in the non-threatening environment of a home.

I believe our children have been greatly enriched by the diversity of people we have had in our home. It's good for their horizons to be widened and to hear testimonies and spiritual conversation from others. This helps them to relate better to different types of people. Children from hospitable families will often surprise their friends with their wide circle of older acquaintances. I remember, when my children were quite young, their head teacher telling me she would often use them to show new families or other visitors around the school, as they were at ease talking to adults and children alike.

There are sometimes quite surprising rewards as a result of hospitality. Once, a notice was given in church that a missionary doctor needed overnight accommodation. Two ladies offered to have her stay with them. One of them had an arm that had been broken but hadn't healed well and, despite various medical interventions, was still causing a lot of problems. The missionary doctor observed this and was able to give advice that provided great relief and increased mobility. To give hospitality to missionaries or a visiting speaker may seem daunting, but the effort is greatly outweighed by the benefit you gain from their experiences and insights.

We can all, therefore, be encouraged by recognizing that there is always blessing in obedience to God's commands. These words of Jesus make this plain: 'If anyone gives a cup of cold water to one of these little ones because he is my disciple, I tell you the truth, he will certainly not lose his reward' (Matthew 10:42).

As we get on with the practice of hospitality, we need to remember that it can be as simple as offering a cup of cold water. That 'cup' might mean boiling the kettle and providing a listening ear. It might mean investing a lot more time and effort. But, whatever form it takes, we do it recognizing that it is a servant ministry to which each one is called by the one who came to serve us. It won't always be easy, it may take effort, but it will be used by God to build up his people as we put into practice what it means to be his body.

ALSO IN THIS SERIES

WISE CHOICES

WHAT THE BIBLE SAYS ABOUT GOING OUT, MARRIAGE AND SEX

CHRIS RICHARDS AND LIZ JONES

God calls us to follow him in every area of our lives, including our sexuality. We were beautifully, delicately, intricately created as sexual beings, but we are so quickly marred when we disregard God's instructions. In a clear biblical and medical framework, two medical doctors sensitively address the matter of relationships.

'Dr Chris Richards and Dr Liz Jones have dared to tell it is as it is, by honestly and frankly explaining what the Bible teaches on sex and relationships.'
ROGER CARSWELL

64PP, BOOKLET, ILLUSTRATED, £3,
ISBN 1 903087 87 2

UNIVERSITY— THE REAL CHALLENGE

ANDREW KING

Is university a good thing for young Christians? Is it a great maturing process, a time of spiritual growth and evangelism? Or is it a time of overwhelming worldly influence, compromise and drifting away from God? Practical pointers to students, parents and churches.

64PP, BOOKLET, ILLUSTRATED, £3,
ISBN 1 903087 82 1